T0145062

NYFW 2021

KATOIA

RUNS THE RUNWAY

Christine Brooks

AuthorHouse™
1663 Liberty Drive
Bloomington, IN 47403
www.authorhouse.com
Phone: 1 (833) 262-8899

Because of the dynamic nature of the Internet, any web addresses or links contained in this book may have changed since publication and may no longer be valid. The views expressed in this work are solely those of the author and do not necessarily reflect the views of the publisher, and the publisher hereby disclaims any responsibility for them.

Any people depicted in stock imagery provided by Getty Images are models, and such images are being used for illustrative purposes only. Certain stock imagery © Getty Images.

This book is printed on acid-free paper.

ISBN: 978-1-6655-0549-9 (sc)
978-1-6655-0548-2 (e)

Print information available on the last page.

Published by AuthorHouse 10/21/2020

authorHOUSE®

KATOIA

RUNS THE RUNWAY

Christine's Clothing Line

By Christine Brooks

2019

HAND IGNITTED
with Rope

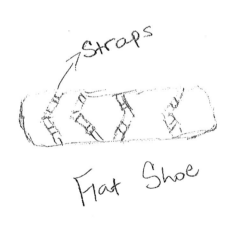

Straps

Flat Shoe

Done by
Ms. Christine Brooks

2o|7

Done by
Ms. Christine Brooks

New 2019

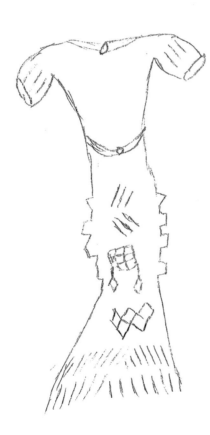

HAND KNITTED

Done by
Ms. Christine Brooks

New
2017

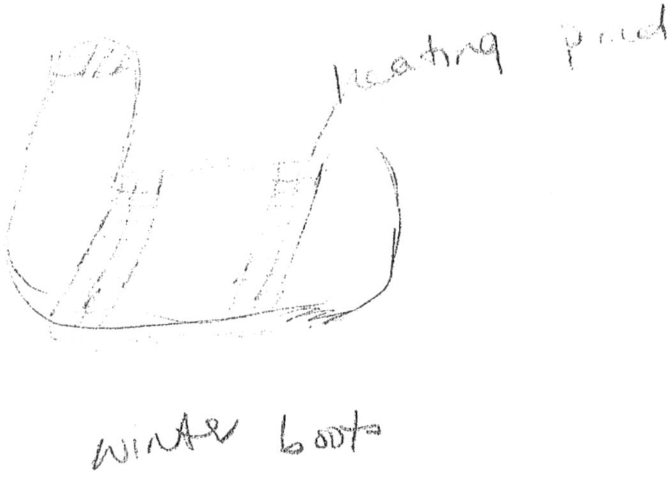

lcating pad

winter boots

Done by
Ms. Christine Brooks

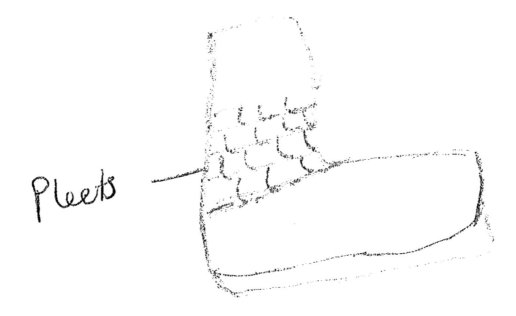

Pleets

boot

Done by

Ms. Christine Brooks

2019   NEW

HAND KNITTED

Done by
Ms. Christine Brooks

NEW 2019

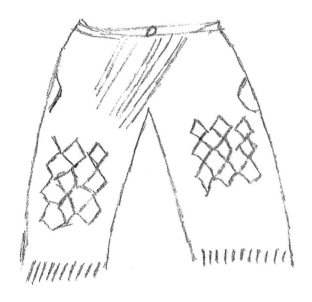

HAND KNITTED

PALAZA PANTS

Done by
Ms. Christine Brooks

2017
Skirt

Done by
Ms. Christine Brooks

NEW 2019

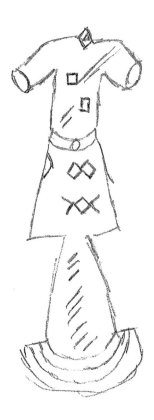

HAND
KNITTED

Done by
Ms. Christine Brooks

2018 NEW

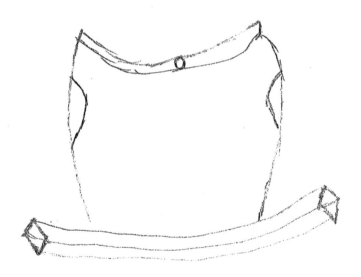

Done by
Ms. Christine Brooks

NEW 2019

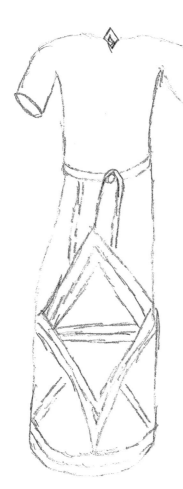

HAND KNITTED

Done by
Ms. Christine Brooks

2018

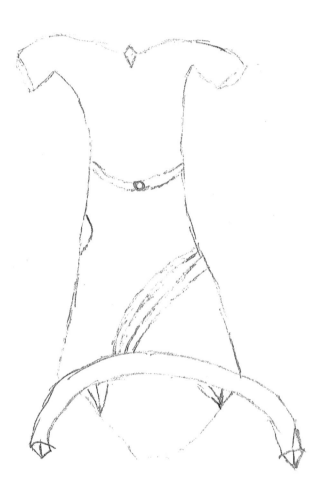

Done by
Ms. Christine Brooks

2018

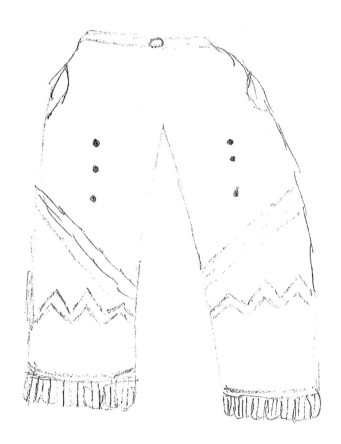

Done by
Ms. Christine Brooks

2019 NEW

HAND KNITTED

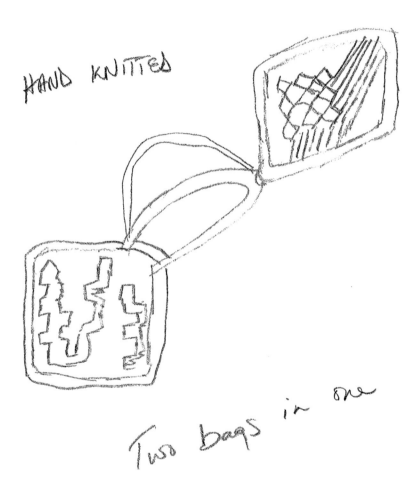

Two bags in one

Done by
Ms. Christine Brooks

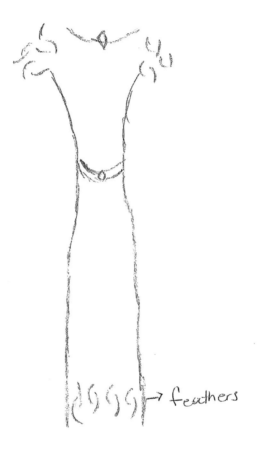

→ feathers

Done by:
Ms Christine
Brooks

Done by
Ms. Christine Brooks

NEW 2019

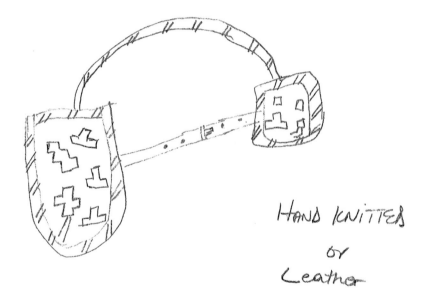

HAND KNITTED
or
Leather

Two Bags in one
with cross buckle

Done by
Ms. Christine Brooks

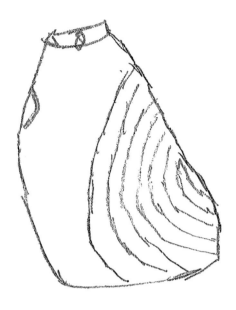

Done by
Ms Christine
Brooks

Done by

Ms. Christine Brooks

2019 New

A Touch of Springtime

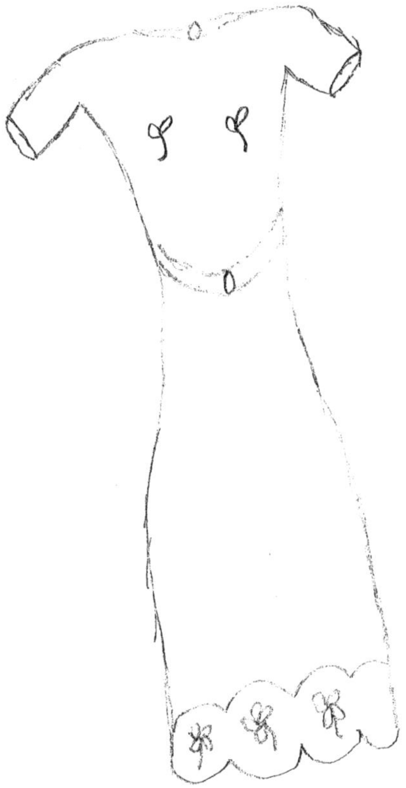

Hand knitted

Done by
Ms. Christine Brooks

Done by
Ms. Christine Brooks

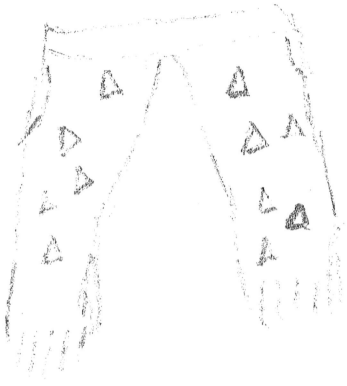

Cores

Palaza Pants

Done by
Ms. Christine Brooks

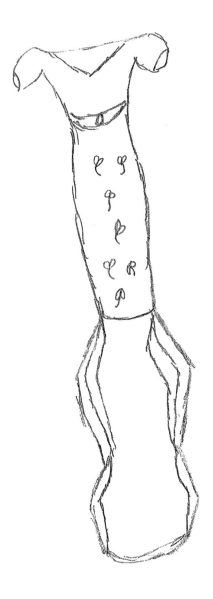

Done by
Ms. Christine Brooks

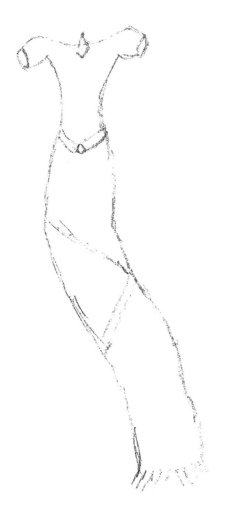

Ballroom Gown

Done by
Ms. Christine Brooks

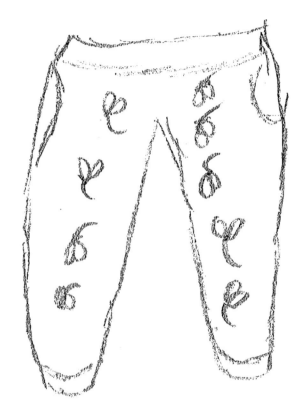

Rose Petals

Done by
Ms. Christine Brooks

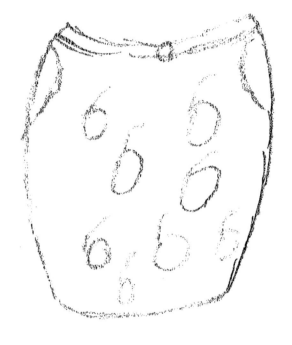

Balloon skirt

Done by
Ms. Christine Brooks

2019
NEW
Hand knitted

PLAIN

Done by
Ms. Christine Brooks

Printed in the United States
By Bookmasters